PREMIERS 20 16 PREMIERS

AGAINST ALL ODDS

A PICTORIAL RECORD OF THE WESTERN BULLDOGS' HISTORY-MAKING SEASON 2016

INTRODUCTION BY PETER GORDON
PHOTOS COURTESY AFL MEDIA AND THE WESTERN BULLDOGS
WORDS BY ANDREW GIGACZ

slattery
MEDIA GROUP

OFFICIAL AFL

www.slatterymedia.com

#BEMORE

BE MORE BULLDOG: 22 Bulldogs form a tight circle and pledge a season-long commitment to the club before the opening bounce of their round one encounter with Fremantle. The Dogs went on to thrash the Dockers—the previous year's minor premiers—to set the tone for the season.

PURE ELATION: With Marcus Bontempelli and Clay Smith about to join him, the look on Tom Liberatore's face says it all as umpire Mathew Nicholls calls a halt to a memorable preliminary final. In front of a near-capacity crowd at the 24,000-seat Spotless Stadium, the Bulldogs came from 14 points behind in the last quarter to record a famous win over Greater Western Sydney and advance to their first Grand Final since 1961.

GUARD OF HONOUR: Bulldogs players triumphantly acknowledge the thanks of thousands of grateful fans as they make their way through the crowd to be presented on stage at the Grand Final after party.

CONTENTS

THE SENSE OF A TEAM, THE FEELING OF A CLUB

The 2016 premiership belongs to the coaching genius of Luke Beveridge.

It belongs to the lonely heroism of Robert Murphy.

It belongs to the unflinching leadership ethic shared by Easton Wood, Rob Murphy, Matthew Boyd, Dale Morris and Marcus Bontempelli, and to the exuberant youthful indomitability 'the Bont' shares with other young blokes... Josh Dunkley, Toby Mclean, Fletcher Roberts, Jake Stringer, Caleb Daniel, Joel Hamling and their mates.

It belongs to the enduring spirit of the Bulldog families: the Liberatores, the Wallises, the Cordys, the Rougheads and the Hunters.

It's embodied in six touches in 30 seconds which made up a desperate Shane Biggs' wall of resistance on the Southern Stand flank that saved the game in the last quarter. It's embodied in the soaring magnificence of Liam Picken's last-quarter grab, a mark now etched forever, like the best of his father's, in the pantheon of great Grand Final moments. It's embodied in the relentless goal kicking accuracy of Tory Dickson.

It belongs to the giant heart of Jordan Roughead.

It belongs to the 60-metre last quarter goal of Jason Johannissen, and to the comical score-review reversal that symbolised to all Bulldogs the frustrations of the past. And it just as surely belongs to another 60-metre game-breaking goal a few minutes later—by Tom Boyd, the young man cruelly dubbed just two years earlier 'the worst trade deal of the millennium'—two 60-metre bombs by the two best players on the ground, making one emphatic statement about the Western Bulldogs.

The 2016 premiership was forged in Clay Smith's return to the team after three knee reconstructions; in Jack Macrae's astonishing finals dominance after a bad hamstring injury just before the final series began; and in Tom Liberatore and Luke Dahlhaus coming back courageously, and too soon, after serious injuries.

The 2016 premiership belongs to all these men and is embodied by all of these moments.

And the 2016 premiership also belongs to us—to you and me.

It belongs to everyone who has ever come to school on footy day and found themselves the only kid in the schoolyard wearing a red, white and blue jumper; to everyone whose heart was broken in any one of seven preliminary final losses.

It belongs to everyone who winced inside when journalists told us that we and our club were irrelevant; or when key people moved on and we were told our club had no trust and no integrity.

It belongs to everyone who died a little inside every time we were told that the club we love and belong to had no legitimate part in a 'truly national competition'; and it belongs to everyone who signed over their pension or rattled a can on a street corner when we were thrown out of the league in 1989.

To understand that our club's history is both tragic and at the same time heroic and precious is to understand the real soul of this club.

The 2016 flag also belongs to every supporter who has confronted their doubts about our club and ultimately about themselves, and dared to believe that, after a lifetime of falling short, something new and profoundly different might be possible.

There will never be a season like 2016; never be another final series remotely the same.

Maybe we will, in our lifetimes, witness another team rise from seventh of the final eight and win the flag.

Maybe before we die, we will see another team travel interstate to win finals in Perth and Sydney and go on to win the premiership.

Maybe we will see another team as young as this one win the flag again; and win despite injury upon crippling injury.

But we will never again see a team that had not graced the MCG on Grand Final day in 55 years, make the Grand Final and win it against all the odds.

This was also a season punctuated by the barnstorming arrivals of Marcus Adams and Zaine Cordy, of Easton Wood taking some of the best marks ever, of the Indian summers in the footy careers of Matt Boyd and Dale Morris—both now premiership players, at last. It was the season of the arrival as elite footballers of Lachie Hunter, Marcus Bontempelli, Tom Liberatore, Luke Dahlhaus, Jack Macrae and Caleb Daniel; and of the revelation, after a career of dour defence, that Liam Picken is an extraordinarily creative footballer with unique offensive flair.

As we limped from the ravages of late 2014, I said at the club's 2015 season launch that how people chose to see the events of October 2014 said as much about us as people as it did the club; I quoted an old saying that a crisis unmasks everyone. I said I chose to see it as the time of the appointment of a great coach, the time of the appointment of one of the great captains of our history and of the assembly of the finest group of young players in the competition. I predicted that in the next few years, people would come to change their weekend plans just to watch us play.

This year, the club has moved from the bottom four, to become—for the first time in its history—the most watched football club in the country.

This has happened because our coaches and our players changed the game.

The club itself is also now changed forever. We look forward with unprecedented confidence to our future in the national league; one club, three teams.

So enjoy the future with our club and be proud of our past. Come back to this book and to 2016 every now and then and tell stories about this unforgettable year to your grandchildren.

When you do, make sure you also tell them that your family belongs to and owns a part of the greatest story in the history of Aussie Rules.

Peter Gordon,
President, Western Bulldogs
October 2016

ADDRESSING THE FAITHFUL: "There will never be a season like 2016; never be another final series remotely the same," wrote Peter Gordon, seen addressing the thousands who came to the Whitten Oval on the day after the premiership drought was broken.

THE ROAD AHEAD

A journey of a thousand kilometres begins with a single step. After unveiling an exciting brand of football under Luke Beveridge, the Bulldogs' 2015 journey ended several steps short of the grand destination, their premiership dream crushed in a heartbreaking loss to Adelaide. It was a season of ultimately unfulfilled ambition, but it had set the foundation for something special.

Players and coaches took several weeks off to reflect and recharge before they reconvened in late December to begin a new journey.

Some players had departed and some new faces appeared. Matt Suckling arrived from Hawthorn, bringing with him premiership experience and a penetrating kick. Via the draft came Marcus Adams, Josh Dunkley, Bailey Williams and Kieran Collins, lacking AFL experience but ready for the journey.

In truth, the journey began not with a step but with a pedal, as the entire group of players and coaches took to the road on bikes to work on aerobic fitness without putting too much weight on their feet. There would be plenty of weight-bearing hard work in the months ahead.

The pre-Christmas training camp was based in Lorne, west of Melbourne along the Great Ocean Road. It gave the players a chance to set goals away from the 'big smoke'. Unexpectedly, it also gave them a chance to reflect on the place football has in life, when smoke of a different sort filled the sky. That smoke came from an out-of-control bushfire in the nearby township of Wye River. The fire razed scores of homes and changed the lives of many. A stark reminder that football—as much as it means to us all—isn't everything.

In the New Year it was back to Whitten Oval, to the weights room, the treadmills, the team meetings, and to the footy field itself. Hours of sweat and toil, planning and preparing, drills and exercises as the journey gained momentum.

By mid-February it was time to test fitness, game plans and mettle as the players went through their strides in the NAB Challenge matches.

Suddenly, it was late March. A round-one match against Fremantle, the 2015 minor premier, beckoned.

The Bulldogs were stepping out on the long road to a premiership.

ALONG FOR THE RIDE: In just two short years since taking over as coach of the Bulldogs, Luke Beveridge has taken players and fans on the ride of a lifetime. In their pre-season camp in and around Lorne, 'Bevo' was only too happy to take on any of the challenges he set for his players. At times he even went the extra mile, as demonstrated when he ran—rather than cycled—alongside Toby McLean. Beveridge took to the road on foot after donating the bike he had been riding to Tom Campbell, whose bicycle had been broken.

**THE FUTURE'S SO BRIGHT
I GOTTA WEAR SHADES:**
Will Minson looks relaxed
as he saddles up for what
would be his last season at
the Kennel. An outstanding
clubman, Minson gave the
Dogs great service in the
ruck across 14 seasons,
reaching a personal pinnacle
in 2013 when he earned
All Australian selection.

STILL IN GOOD SHAPE: Dressed for a pre-season bike ride with the players, Daniel Giansiracusa still looks as though he could mix it with the AFL's best on the field. The team's premiership forward coach, 'Gia' will take over the 'stoppages and set plays' portfolio for the 2017 season.

CALL TO ARMS: Inducted into the Bulldogs' leadership group for the first time in the 2016 pre-season, Easton Wood was thrust into the captaincy role far earlier than he would have anticipated, elevated to the role after Bob Murphy's season-ending knee injury in round three.

QUICK HANDS: Marcus Bontempelli and Kieran Collins are a picture of concentration during a handball drill. The Bulldogs' superior use of the ball by hand was identified by many pundits as a key to the team's 2016 success, invoking memories of the 'flick pass', used to great effect by Ted Whitten's Bulldogs in the season the Dogs last made a Grand Final, 1961.

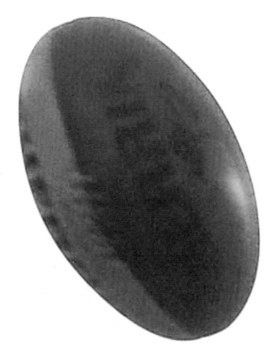

GREAT EXPECTATIONS: The inevitable expectations that come with being a number one draft pick and a after much-scrutinised switch from GWS to the Bulldogs were always a weight that Tom Boyd would have to bear. Boyd's season was interrupted by a shoulder injury but he returned to make a vital contribution throughout the finals, firstly when asked to carry the ruck work in the preliminary final when Jordan Roughead was struck down and then, as a big forward, on Grand Final day.

WITHIN REACH OF A FLAG: The prospect of playing finals, let alone a Grand Final, can appear a long way off during the arduous pre-season but a premiership at the end of a lengthy campaign made all the hard work and meticulous preparation worth it for Caleb Daniel and his teammates.

AT A STRETCH: Despite being
hampered throughout the season
by an achilles complaint that saw
him miss nine matches, including
the Grand Final, Matt Suckling's
accurate, penetrating kicks
helped add a new dimension
to the Bulldogs' back six in 2016.
He does have some consolation:
two Premiership Medals gained
with Hawthorn in 2014/15.

**EMERGING FROM THE
SHADOWS:** Once seen as an
effective run-with player with no
other strings to his bow, Liam Picken
has blossomed in his late 20s as
a freewheeling, high-marking player
who is very dangerous around goal.

WESTERN BULLDOGS

CRISIS AND OPPORTUNITY

The Chinese word for 'crisis' and 'opportunity' is supposedly one and the same. Whatever the truth of that notion, the Western Bulldogs faced numerous moments during the home-and-away season that could be described as crises—almost all of them injury-related—and turned them into opportunities.

Crisis number one came early in the season. In round three, the Bulldogs came into their match against Hawthorn, the reigning premier, undefeated. Late in the game the Dogs led narrowly and victory was at hand when the Hawks stormed forward. In the final marking contest of the match, Hawk James Sicily grabbed the ball as Bob Murphy grabbed his knee.

The next moment brought two heartbreaks. Sicily kicked a long goal to seal a gut-wrenching three-point loss, but an event that would resonate throughout the entire season was unfolding metres away as Sicily was lining up. Captain Bob had ruptured an ACL. The Bulldogs had lost to Hawthorn in a mighty battle but, more seriously, had lost their skipper—the club's spiritual leader—for the season. Perhaps for good.

How the Bulldogs reacted to that moment would be a key to the remainder of their season. Some pundits claimed that the Dogs' premiership hopes ended the moment Murphy's knee gave way. But Luke Beveridge and his charges would have none of that. The Dogs bounced back to beat the Blues the following week, although that match, too, brought its own crisis, with Jason Johannisen severely tearing a hamstring as he kicked a long goal.

He would not return until round 15, at which point he would provide another key moment in the Bulldogs' season, kicking a goal virtually on the siren to give the Dogs victory over Sydney at the SCG for the second year running. Some had seen the equally close away win over the Swans in 2015 as lucky, but a second victory there confirmed this Bulldogs side as a force.

Crises and opportunities flowed freely, with Jack Redpath and Mitch Wallis lost to season-ending leg injuries in round 18, and Tom Liberatore and Jack Macrae to ankle and hamstring injuries the next week. Again the Dogs turned despair into hope, with Joel Hamling and Fletcher Roberts among those to come in and fill the breaches. A week after 'Libba' and Macrae went down, the Dogs returned to the winners' list with a fighting effort over North Melbourne.

Perhaps the most significant of the Bulldogs' key moments in 2016 came on the eve of the finals. It was significant for two reasons, both of which arose as the result of the AFL's creative move to introduce a week off between the end of the home-and-away season and the first week of finals.

This first allowed the league to showcase the finest female footballers in the land, with an exhibition match played at Whitten Oval on the 'bye' Saturday night drawing a great crowd and a huge television audience. It was a magnificent spectacle, made all the better for the faithful as the Bulldogs easily beat Melbourne.

The 'bye' week also gave several key players the extra time they needed to recover from injury. With finals upon them, Tom Liberatore, Jack Macrae, Easton Wood and Jordan Roughead were fit, firing and about to join their teammates in playing major roles in an unforgettable month of football.

GAME PLAN: Dale Morris watches and listens intently as Luke Beveridge goes through some finer points of the Bulldogs' strategy. Although Beveridge has a coaching style all of his own, there's no doubt his time as an assistant coach at Hawthorn taught him the value of a game plan that allows one fallen 'soldier' to be replaced by another in any given role.

THIS IS IT BOYS: Having started the season with two big wins, round three gave the Bulldogs a chance to test themselves against the best—reigning premier Hawthorn. The Dogs led by 19 points at the last change but the never-say-die Hawks came back to steal a three-point win at the death. This would be the last time in 2016 that Bob Murphy would lead his charges into battle, a knee injury just before the final siren ending his season.

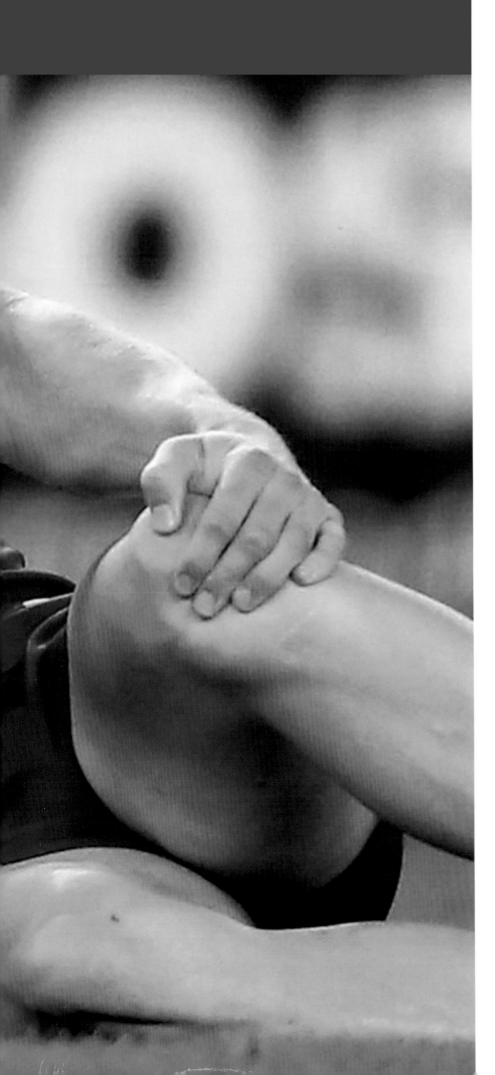

DESPAIR: A thrilling clash with Hawthorn in round three ended in the worst possible way for the Bulldogs when skipper Bob Murphy's knee gave way in the dying seconds of the match. Later diagnosed with a ruptured ACL, Murphy would miss the rest of the season. To rub salt into the wound, a late goal to James Sicily moments after Murphy went down saw the Bulldogs lose to the Hawks by three points.

BRUSHING OFF THE BLUES: Playing his first game in the red, white and blue, former Brisbane captain Jed Adcock celebrated by kicking a goal early in the first quarter as he helped the Bulldogs to a solid six-goal round-four win over Carlton. It was an encouraging response to the heartbreaking loss to Hawthorn (and the loss of Bob Murphy for the season) a week earlier. The win lifted the Dogs back up to second on the ladder. Adcock retired at the end of the season, having joined the Bulldogs as a rookie in 2016 after 12 seasons with Brisbane.

WE WILL BE STRONG: Luke Dahlhaus celebrates a goal against North Melbourne in round six. Dahlhaus was a model of consistency once more in 2016, burrowing under packs to rack up contested possessions almost at will. He regularly featured in the best players and collected seven Brownlow votes, a figure that undoubtedly would have been higher had he not missed five games with a knee injury. He had 23 touches and laid eight tackles in the Grand Final win.

YOU'RE NOT GOING ANYWHERE: Caleb Daniel and Tom Liberatore make sure Melbourne's Jack Viney doesn't get away with a clean disposal, providing a fine example of the Bulldogs' characteristically ferocious attack on the ball—or the man with the ball—in 2016. For 'Libba', this was one of 19 tackles he laid in the round-eight match against the Demons, equalling the record set by North's Jack Ziebell earlier in the year and by Sydney's Jude Bolton in 2011.

THE AGONY: Sadly, the Bulldogs' serious injury woes did not end with Bob Murphy and Jason Johannisen in rounds three and four. In round 18, a dirty Saturday night for the Dogs ended not only with an unexpected loss to the Saints but also the loss of Jack Redpath and Mitch Wallis to long-term leg injuries. Redpath suffered his third ruptured ACL while Wallis sustained breaks to both his fibula and tibia in a horrific accident in the last quarter. Wallis' immense pain was immediately obvious and lasted until well after the end of the match, his haunting screams in the rooms moving many of his teammates to tears.

PUTTING ON THE CLAMPS:
Three wins in row from West Coast
saw the Eagles sneak ahead of
the Bulldogs on the ladder before
the sides met at Etihad Stadium in
round 11. In a high-quality match
played with finals-like intensity, the
Bulldogs displayed great ferocity
and endeavour, exemplified by this
Jake Stringer tackle on Andrew
Gaff, to halt the Eagles' run and
go on to win by eight points.

THE RED, WHITE AND BLUE PATH TO VICTORY: Jack Redpath celebrates one of the four goals he kicked against Port Adelaide in round 12. Redpath played a vital role in getting the Dogs over the line by just three points, the narrow win keeping the team inside the top four. His season ended prematurely with a knee injury in round 18, but Redpath played a major part in the Dogs' charge to a flag in his 10 matches in 2016.

READY-MADE DEFENDER: Joining the Western Bulldogs as a mature-age recruit from West Perth, Marcus Adams impressed enough in the pre-season to make his debut in round one against Fremantle. He looked immediately at home and made the full-back position his own, taking 15 marks in just his third AFL game against Hawthorn, but finger, leg and shoulder injuries would ultimately see his season end prematurely in July.

ROUGHEAD'S DAY IN THE SUN:
Jordan Roughead walked off the
Adelaide Oval a happy man after
his 100th AFL match, a thrilling
three-point win over Port Adelaide.
The big man played an important
rucking role in the win, collecting
29 hitouts to go with his
12 possessions.

CRASH! The Bulldogs were travelling nicely as they headed into their round 13 clash with Geelong—with a place in the top two up for grabs—but they crashed headlong into a Cats' line-up that barely put a foot wrong. The Cats were dominant, leaving Matt Suckling and his teammates with battered bodies and bruised egos.

FIRST ONE'S A CHARM: Having missed 12 weeks with a serious hamstring tear, Jason Johanissen made every post a winner in his first game back against Sydney in round 15, collecting 20 touches and laying four tackles off a half-back flank. Not content with that, 'JJ' sneaked forward in the dying seconds of the match to accept a pass from Marcus Bontempelli and calmly slot through a goal that gave the Bulldogs a thrilling four-point victory, one which put the Dogs' season back on track after a heavy loss to Geelong in their previous game.

FISTS OF FURY: The Bulldogs won 15 games in the home-and-away season, but victories didn't always come easily. Richmond led the Dogs early in the final term of their round 16 match and Easton Wood and his fellow defenders had to work hard to spoil the Tigers' party. Their efforts and some late magic from Jake 'The Package' Stringer saw the Bulldogs get over the line by 10 points.

ALL CLEAR: Umpire Sam Hay signals a goal as Jake Stringer's eyes are drawn to his teammates after he has kicked a vital goal against Richmond. The Bulldogs struggled for much of their round 16 match against the Tigers and were still trailing by a point as late as 23 minutes into the final term. But two late goals from 'The Package' saw the Bulldogs home, as they continued to enhance their reputation of being able to find a way to win the close ones. Stringer had been quiet in the first half but his four majors after the long break were a big factor in the Dogs getting over the line.

HUNTER BECOMES THE HUNTED: Lachie Hunter, with trademark curling tongue protruding, gets a kick away under extreme pressure from Saint Nathan Wright. The Dogs were riding high in third place on the table going into their round 18 clash against St Kilda, but they came up against a fierce Saints outfit that hunted and ran in numbers. Despite Hunter continuing his fine season with a 28-possession game, the Dogs went down by 15 points, with serious leg injuries to Mitch Wallis and Jack Redpath making a dirty night much dirtier.

RUING A MISSED OPPORTUNITY: Many things didn't go to plan for the Bulldogs as they travelled the road to a premiership. A win against St Kilda in round 18 would have seen the Dogs secure outright second place on the ladder but virtually nothing went right on the night. The Bulldogs lost the match, and Mitch Wallis and Jack Redpath to season-ending injuries, leaving the players to rue what might have been.

PRAISE THE BOYD: The Bulldogs' annual trip to Cairns for a 'home' game against Gold Coast saw Tom Boyd return to the side after a 13-week layoff, courtesy of a shoulder injury and a club-enforced suspension. Boyd had a relatively quiet night as the Dogs recorded an eight-goal win, but his goal just after half-time saw his teammates demonstrate how glad they were to see him back. Boyd went on to become a critical component in the Bulldogs' quest for the flag.

WE'RE ALL IN THIS TOGETHER: The Bulldogs banded together to bounce back from injury setbacks and two consecutive losses to post a gutsy win over North Melbourne in round 20. The players wore Cookie Monster socks for the match, in support of the Children's Cancer Foundation.

SUCCESS BREEDS SUCCESS: Setting the tone for the rest of the finals series, the Western Bulldogs defeated Melbourne in the Women's All Star exhibition match played on the 'bye' weekend after the home-and-away season. Celebrating with Western Bulldogs board member and long-time advocate of women's football Susan Alberti are:

BACK (L-R): Ellyse Gamble, Bianca Jakobsson, Nicola Barr, Emma King, Brianna Davey, Leah Kaslar
CENTRE (L-R): Moana Hope, Maddy Collier, Emma Kearney, Emma Humphries, Jaimee Lambert, Emily Bates, Katie Brennan, Steph Ciocci, Richelle Cranston, Darcy Vescio
FRONT (L-R): Maddy Keryk, Ellie Blackburn, Kaitlyn Ashmore, Lauren Arnell, Tahllia Randall, Nicola Stevens, Hannah Scott

AGAINST ALL ODDS

The early part of October in 2014 was a time of unrest at the Western Bulldogs. For a club that has seen more than its fair share of turmoil, this period was up there as one of the most tumultuous.

The upheaval climaxed on October 10 when coach Brendan McCartney tendered his resignation to the Western Bulldogs board. A day earlier, captain Ryan Griffen had requested a trade to Greater Western Sydney, citing irreconcilable differences with the coach.

After McCartney's resignation, president Peter Gordon revealed that a post-season review had showed the coach's communication with players had become a serious issue in the second half of 2014. It all seemed quite hopeless—from the outside at least.

Fast forward two years to the early days of October 2016. Days of unrest had been replaced by days of jubilation. In 24 short months, the Western Bulldogs had transformed from a club seemingly on the brink to the reigning AFL premiers.

Under the guidance of coach Luke Beveridge and the captaincy of Bob Murphy—both appointed in the aftermath of the upheaval of 2014—the Bulldogs made a dramatic rise in 2015, reaching the finals and falling just short of Adelaide in a frenzied elimination final that many described as the best match of the season.

The appointments of 'Bevo' and Bob would prove to be not only popular but among the most astute in the history of a club that has tasted little success in the 91 years since it joined the VFL in 1925, as the reigning premier of the VFA (the "Association").

After 2015's great leap forward, 2016 dawned full of hope for the Western Bulldogs. There were some who doubted that the Dogs could back up the promising efforts of the season before, reflecting, no doubt, on the rise and fall of Port Adelaide (preliminary finalist in 2014, ninth the following year). "They took all by surprise last year, the other clubs will have worked them out by now," claimed a chorus of 'experts'.

But Beveridge, his coaching panel and his players would hear none of that. He knew that the young Bulldogs' list was one that featured sublime talent and great depth. He also felt very confident that he had devised a game plan that all 44 players on the list would buy into and would stand up against the best the others had to offer.

There would be hurdles throughout the season, as injury after injury hit every line—some of them seemingly insurmountable. The first came in round three when

Murphy's knee gave way in the dying seconds of the heartbreaking three-point loss to Hawthorn.

But there were more to come. Jason Johannisen tore the hamstring off his bone in round four, surely a season-ending calamity. Matt Suckling had achilles troubles throughout the season. Marcus Adams also fell foul of the injury gods. At times it seemed as though the Dogs' best back six was either on the sidelines or hobbling.

It didn't end there. In round 18, Jack Redpath and Mitch Wallis were lost to serious leg injuries. The following week, Tom Liberatore and Jack Macrae went down. Surely, there could be no overcoming such adversity.

Beveridge would not be deterred: "Try telling the players that," he said. He continued to believe, in his players—all of them on the list—and in his game plan. In the end, his belief was vindicated. When 'first choice' players were unavailable, others stepped up to fill the breach, some making themselves 'first choice' players in the process.

The Bulldogs kept winning more often than not, the team-first plan surviving test after test. Of course there were losses along the way, but, with just one exception, they were generally narrow. When the going got tough, the Bulldogs knew what to do. After the round-three loss to the Hawks, they played in five more matches decided by under 10 points and won them all.

Fifteen wins, enough to earn a top-four place in six of the previous 10 seasons, saw the Bulldogs finish seventh, a position from which no team had ever won a flag. More fascinating is the fact that since the final eight was introduced in 1994, only six teams have won more than 12 matches and finished seventh, with Fremantle's 14 wins in 2012 the best performed. That too was of no concern to 'Bevo' and his Bulldogs, particularly with the AFL's inclusion of a bye after round 23 for the finalists. With several players making a welcome return from injury, the Dogs made five significant changes to their team for the elimination final, and were ready to mount a challenge. In came Tom Liberatore, Jack Macrae, Jordan Roughead, Jake Stringer and Easton Wood.

Against all odds, they travelled to Perth and eliminated the Eagles. Against all odds, they took on the might of the Hawks—undisputed champions for three long years—and defeated them. Against all odds, they travelled to Sydney and slayed the star-studded GWS Giants to become the first Victorian side to win interstate twice in one finals campaign. Against all odds, the Bulldogs had broken the preliminary final curse to make a Grand Final for the first time in five-and-a-half decades.

YES! It was his first final and only his 14th AFL match but Josh Dunkley showed no signs of nerves in the game against West Coast in Subiaco. He kicked two goals, had 15 touches, laid four tackles and even had three hitouts as a 'third-up' ruckman, to help the Dogs to a momentous win.

BEATEN NECK AND CROP:
The Eagles went into the second
elimination final as hot favourites
on their home turf but the Bulldogs
shrugged them off to win by
47 points, with a manic mixture
of contested and free-flowing
football that would be a feature
throughout the finals series.

DELIGHT AND DESPAIR:
The Bulldogs' against-the-odds win
against West Coast in the second
elimination final was cause for great
celebration for most, but it was a
bittersweet occasion for Lin Jong,
who broke his collarbone during
the match. Here, he is consoled
by club doctor Gary Zimmermann.

A WIN FOR ALL TO SHARE:
Easton Wood is cock-a-hoop with
the Bulldogs' win over West Coast
at Subiaco in the elimination final,
as are the coaching staff (from left),
Steven King, Rohan Smith, Graham
Lowe and Chris Maple. Smith's 300th
and final AFL match for the Bulldogs
was a semi-final loss to the Eagles
at the same venue in 2006.

GATHER THE PACK:
On a fine September evening, Bulldogs fans marched as one from Federation Square to the MCG to see their team take on the might of Hawthorn, the reigning premier. They were in for a special treat.

A TOUCHING MOMENT: Toby McLean celebrates what he thinks is a goal but Hawk skipper Luke Hodge is convinced he's touched the ball off the boot. Hodge was right. After the goal umpire had signalled a major, the video umpire overturned the decision. Ultimately, it did not matter, with the Bulldogs winning the second semi-final by 23 points.

A HAIR-RAISING AFFAIR:
Bulldogs fans who have witnessed
seven preliminary final losses
since the Dogs' last Grand Final
appearance in 1961 were kept in
suspense until the very end of
2016's penultimate match. The
Bulldogs lost Jordan Roughead—
pictured taking an early mark—
to an eye injury in the second
term, courtesy of a ball to
the face kicked from close
range. With Tom Boyd manfully
shouldering the ruck duties for
the rest of the match, they eked
out a thrilling six-point win to
break the preliminary-final curse.

SLAYING THE GIANT: Coach Luke Beveridge might have given Liam Picken a new lease on life by playing him forward but in the preliminary final he demonstrated that his defensive skills are as good as ever with this tackle on GWS's Dylan Shiel.

REMEMBER ME? Tom Boyd locks horns with Greater Western Sydney's Shane Mumford in the preliminary final. The two were teammates at GWS in Boyd's first AFL season. Boyd did a sterling job in the ruck after Jordan Roughead was forced out of the game with an eye injury in the second quarter.

GIANT STEP FORWARD: After making some uncharacteristic errors in the first half of the preliminary final, Caleb Daniel was a pivotal player for the Bulldogs in the second, his goal just before three-quarter time bringing the Dogs to within a point of GWS at the last break.

TEAM DEFENCE: Shane Biggs, Fletcher Roberts, Joel Hamling and Tom Boyd (hidden) combine to thwart another GWS forward foray in the preliminary final. Team defence was a feature of the Bulldogs' 2016 back half, stretched to the limit by a run of injuries to key defenders throughout the season.

IT'S BEEN A WHILE: Jack Macrae (right) and Luke Dahlhaus celebrate the goal that gave the Bulldogs victory against Greater Western Sydney. Macrae's first major since round one put the Dogs into their first Grand Final in 55 years.

SMILE! Tory Dickson has good reason to be happy, even before he takes the last kick of the preliminary final. The final siren had sounded with the Bulldogs five points ahead of GWS. Dickson's shot hit the post, making the Dogs' winning margin six points.

I'M SO HAPPY I COULD KISS YOU: Marcus Bontempelli and Luke Beveridge share a special moment after the Bulldogs' preliminary final. 'The Bont' kicked a vital last-quarter goal to give the Dogs a lead they would not relinquish.

I'M BACK: Barely more than two weeks after breaking his collarbone in the elimination final, Lin Jong was back playing for the Bulldogs in the VFL Grand Final. He showed no signs of discomfort and put his hand up for AFL Grand Final selection with a best-on-ground performance that earned him the Norm Goss Memorial Medal.

PREMIERSHIP DEPTH: Coach Ashley Hansen and captain Jordan Russell hold the premiership cup aloft after the Bulldogs defeated Casey to win the VFL flag. The Bulldogs also won the 2014 VFL premiership, an indicator of the depth of talent the club has developed over the past few years. Much of that depth is attributable to the fine work done by recruiting manager Simon Dalrymple and list manager Jason McCartney, who have combined brilliantly to put together an array of talent and character that should see the Bulldogs continue to be a force for years to come.

THE STADIUM HOLDS ITS BREATH

Saturday, October 1, 2016, dawned fine and still. This was a day many long-suffering Bulldogs fans thought would never come. As the sun rose over Melbourne, the city began to fill with footy lovers, the Footscray faithful dominant among them. By mid-morning there was no escaping an eyeful of red, white and blue, no matter which direction you faced. There was also a sprinkling of red and white, with many fans of the Sydney Swans—formerly South Melbourne—no strangers to this town.

But the force was with the Bulldogs as their legion of fans calmed pre-match nerves with breakfast and drinks before making the trek to the 'G for the big match.

Mike Brady, Sting, Vance Joy and Vika and Linda Bull displayed their musical talent in the lead-up to the opening bounce. Many Bulldogs fans—and certainly the players—would barely have taken in the entertainment, their only focus the game ahead.

The match was one for the ages. The intensity in the first 10 minutes was as fierce as one will ever see on a football field, as the players bashed and crashed into each other, asking and giving no quarter in their efforts to be first to the ball.

Mistakes abounded, some born of nerves, others from the breathtaking pressure applied by the opposition. Eventually the players settled, Sydney's first, with Swan Luke Parker scoring the Grand Final's first goal after 12 feverish minutes.

Finally, on the cusp of time-on, a vice-like tackle on Rising Star winner Callum Mills by Zaine Cordy was rewarded with a free kick. Cordy's long kick from the boundary line negotiated the swirling breeze beautifully and the Bulldogs were away. Soon after Tory Dickson marked and kicked one of his typically gun-barrel straight goals and the Dogs were in front— by four points—at the first break.

The intensity did not wane in the second term, but goals began to flow. Four were scored in the first 12 minutes, with Bulldogs Tom Boyd, Dickson and Liam Picken kicking three of them. Suddenly the Dogs were 16 points ahead and the prospect of a premiership seemed very, very real.

But with Josh Kennedy playing a starring role, Sydney slammed on four goals to regain the lead by eight points. This was one of the Grand Final's moments of truth, and the Bulldogs responded, kicking two of the next three goals, with Tom Boyd again making a statement and Toby McLean snaring a vital major with a clever snap just before the half-time siren.

If it were possible, the manic intensity went up a notch in the third quarter. Dickson bobbed up with his third four minutes into the term to give the Dogs the lead, but goals were few and fair between for the remainder of the quarter. Kennedy continued to stamp himself on the game and his third goal returned the lead to Sydney.

Just before the clock ticked over into time-on, Clay Smith was taken high and he kicked truly with the resultant free kick. The Bulldogs were ahead once more and for the rest of the quarter they mounted repeated attacks without a goal. Caleb Daniel, Jake Stringer and Tom Boyd all had shots. All missed. The three-quarter time siren sounded and the final break of the 2016 season saw the Bulldogs eight points ahead, and 30 minutes from glory.

Again, the early stages of the final term had both teams attacking with frenzied hunger. Again, goals proved to be rare. The first of the final quarter came at the seven-minute mark, when Lance Franklin kicked a classic 'Buddy' goal from the boundary line to bring Sydney within a point.

Liam Picken provided a highlight for the ages with a screamer on the forward line. His brilliant mark didn't result in a goal, but not long after Jake Stringer, well held by Dane Rampe, seized a rare moment of freedom to take a loose ball and a snap a goal, restoring a seven-point lead for the Dogs. The margin was back to a point with George Hewett goaling for Sydney soon after.

Midway through the term with the ball pin-balling between players on the Bulldogs' half-forward line, Shane Biggs got his hands to it an amazing six times in 30 seconds, doing everything possible to prevent Sydney from sweeping the ball away. His heroic efforts were rewarded when the ball eventually came loose and found its way to Picken, whose snapped goal extended the margin again to seven points.

The Bulldogs were nearly home but they needed one special piece of magic to ensure the premiership cup would be theirs.

Enter Tom Boyd.

Having already made a significant impact on the Grand Final, he swooped on a loose ball, forced free from Franklin's hands by a crunching tackle from—who else?—Dale Morris. Boyd gave the ball everything he could with his right boot from inside the centre square. The ball pitched in the goal square and seemed to pause in a moment captured perfectly by Channel 7's Denis Cometti in his AFL swansong: "The stadium holds its breath."

The ball continued on its path, bisecting the goalposts, and the stadium breathed again. And then screamed out. The Bulldogs were 15 points ahead in time-on of the Grand Final and their fans knew that a 62-year drought was about to end.

Picken made certain of it four minutes later with his third goal. The siren sounded soon after, the scoreboard showing the Dogs 22 points ahead. Twenty-two players raised both arms to the heavens. They had done it.

In just two short years, Luke Beveridge had taken this team to a height not reached since 1954, when Charlie Sutton and Ted Whitten led the Bulldogs to their first flag after 30 seasons in the league. As Beveridge, Bob Murphy, Easton Wood and all the players beamed, smiling the smiles that belong only to the victors, it was not hard to imagine Charlie and E.J. beaming down on them from above and smiling with them.

JUST LIKE BILLY: Midway through the final term of the Grand Final, Liam Picken flew majestically through the air to take 'screamer' over Swan Jeremy Laidler, echoing the many great marks taken by his father Billy for Collingwood. While Billy never tasted premiership success, playing in five Grand Finals without a win, Liam has achieved the ultimate. Previously renowned as a dour tagger, the younger Picken has flourished as a midfielder and forward since being granted freedom to run and play his own game under coach Luke Beveridge.

WE'RE IN THE GRAND FINAL? YOU'RE JOKING! He may have had some serious preparation work to do in the lead-up to the big day, but Luke Beveridge still found time for a laugh during the Bulldogs' final training session before the Grand Final.

LOOK WHO'S BOBBED UP: Already in very good spirits in the lead-up to the club's biggest match in more than 50 years, the mood of players and fans was buoyed further by the sight of Bob Murphy—well on the road to a full recovery from his round-three knee injury—having a run at the last training session before the Grand Final.

ARTHUR OLLIVER

JUST LIKE OLD TIMES: The E.J. Whitten stand is rarely filled these days but the fans were out in force to see the Bulldogs go through their final paces in preparation for the Grand Final under the names of Bulldog legends Arthur Olliver, Charlie Sutton and John Schultz.

TICKETS PLEASE: With most of Melbourne getting behind the Bulldogs in the lead-up to the Grand Final, spare tickets to the big game were as rare as hen's teeth. This ambitious Dogs' fan tried his luck outside the MCG before the match. The final attendance was only 19 short of 100,000.

CALM BEFORE THE STORM:
A look towards the Punt Road goals early on the morning of the 2016 Grand Final. When the Bulldogs last took to the MCG in a Grand Final in 1961, club logos painted in the turf were unheard of. Even the 50-metre arc was more than two decades away from being introduced.

IT IS WRITTEN: After a season of lighthearted banners penned by comedian Danny McGinlay, a slightly more serious tone was adopted for the Grand Final: "WE'VE BEATEN ALL THE OTHERS, DEFIED ALL THE ODDS, TODAY THIS TEAM OF PUPPIES BECOME TRUE BULLGODS!"

BEFORE THE BATTLE: A relatively recent innovation, the pre-game, on-field team photo captures forever the nervous smiles and many looks of fierce determination that adorn the faces of the players as they prepare to head into the battle of a lifetime.

Back row (L-R): Joel Hamling, Toby McLean, Jack Macrae, Liam Picken, Clay Smith, Tom Boyd, Jordan Roughead, Fletcher Roberts, Zaine Cordy, Tom Liberatore, Shane Biggs, Jake Stringer, Josh Dunkley.

Front row (L-R): Luke Dahlhaus, Tory Dickson, Dale Morris, Marcus Bontempelli, Luke Beveridge (coach), Easton Wood (captain), Caleb Daniel, Lachie Hunter, Matthew Boyd, Jason Johannisen.

PUT YOUR MONEY ON THE DOGS: With a look of steely determination, Easton Wood walks to the centre of the MCG for the coin toss. Wood won the toss, and the Bulldogs went on to win the premiership.

PLUCK THE SWANS: A passionate fan holds up a banner that reflected the attitude—if not the exact words—of all Bulldogs and most neutral fans at the MCG on Grand Final day. Politically incorrect, or a quality forecast, or both?

OLD RELIABLE: Tory Dickson has become renowned for his set-shot accuracy in front of goal. It deserted him briefly in the semi-final, but he got the Bulldogs off to a great start with this kick in the first quarter of the Grand Final. He finished the day with 3.0.

EYES ON THE PRIZE: Zaine Cordy might not have been the youngest player on the field on Grand Final day (teammate Josh Dunkley and Sydney's Callum Mills are several months younger) but he was the most inexperienced, the premiership decider being just his 11th match. The son of former Footscray player Brian Cordy played two games late in 2015 as a defender and rejoined the side in round 19 this year against Geelong as a 'defensive' forward. Cordy has not been a high-possession winner in his 12 games but his straight-ahead attack on the ball or the man with the ball played a vital role in keeping possession in the Dogs' forward line through the finals. He also kicked two important goals in the preliminary final and sent the Bulldogs on the path to glory with the first goal of the Grand Final, a reward for a crunching tackle on Callum Mills.

THE EYES HAVE IT: Jordan Roughead and Swan Kurt Tippett lock arms in the Grand Final. Roughead and Tom Boyd have blossomed as an alternating ruck-forward combination in 2016. They combined to have 31 hitouts in the Grand Final.

A FLAG WITHIN REACH: They say that being an AFL footballer requires a back-breaking effort but Dale Morris might have taken that old adage too literally! After his Grand Final heroics (15 possessions, countless 'one-percenters' and the tackle on Lance Franklin that resulted in the Tom Boyd goal that broke the back of the Swans), Morris revealed that he had broken two vertebrae in his back in the round 23 loss to Fremantle. However, with a premiership at stake, nothing was going to stop 'Mozz' from playing though the finals, regardless of the injury. He said after the match, "I may have (broken my back) in the last game against Freo, but who cares now!"

A PLUCKY EFFORT: Jason Johannisen just about did it all on Grand Final day, his Norm Smith Medal-winning performance consisting of 25 kicks, eight handballs and seven timely marks such as this one, which saw him outreach the taller Dan Hannebery from behind. 'JJ' polled 10 votes in the medal count to finish two clear of Sydney's Josh Kennedy, with Tom Boyd polling seven and Liam Picken five.

OUT OF TROUBLE: Fletcher Roberts may have had only five possessions in the Grand Final, but his spoils and pressure acts ensured that the Swans rarely had an easy possession in their forward line. Roberts' fine defensive efforts in the preliminary final when he came into replace the injured Matt Suckling saw him retain his place in the side for the biggest match of the year.

GRAND FINAL

GOTCHA! Shane Biggs ensures that Sydney Rising Star Callum Mills is going nowhere during the Grand Final. Traded from Sydney at the end of the 2014 season, Biggs took some time to find his feet and a regular place in the Bulldogs' best 22, but a breakout game against Collingwood in round 17 last season saw him cement himself as a permanent member of the team. Late in the last quarter of the Grand Final, Biggs displayed great heroism, getting his hand on the ball no fewer than six times in 30 seconds to ensure it didn't escape from the Dogs' forward line. The ball landed in the arms of Liam Picken soon after, and his second goal went a long way to ensuring Grand Final victory.

DEADEYE DICKSON: Tory Dickson celebrates another Grand Final goal with Lachie Hunter. Dickson kicked three vital goals in the Grand Final, and his uncanny accuracy when lining up is a feature of his game. That accuracy deserted him briefly in the semi-final against Hawthorn, but his 4.1 against GWS in the preliminary final, and 3.0 in the final game went a long way towards helping the Bulldogs break the premiership drought.

A LEAP OF FAITH: With Lin Jong succumbing to a collarbone injury in the Dogs' elimination final win at Subiaco, Toby McLean was called to fill the breach. The lightly-built McLean slotted into the gap perfectly, collecting more than 20 touches in the semi and preliminary finals. Jong made a remarkable recovery to be available for the Grand Final—winning the Norm Goss Memorial Medal for best afield in the VFL Grand Final a week earlier—but McLean's efforts warranted him keeping his place on the big day. McLean rewarded the selectors' faith with a solid performance and kicked a critical goal just before the half-time break to the keep the Dogs in touch with Sydney.

HANG ON, BUDDY: Joel Hamling would be the first to admit that he was little more than a bit-part player for the Bulldogs for the bulk of his two seasons at the Kennel, but he was outstanding in defence throughout the 2016 finals series, his job curbing Lance Franklin playing a huge part in the Dogs' Grand Final victory.

I CAN DO THIS WITH MY EYES CLOSED: Jordan Roughead's contested marking was a key component of the Bulldogs' success throughout the finals. This grab over teammate Marcus Bontempelli and Swan Heath Grundy was one of five he took on Grand Final day.

WE'VE GOT YOUR MEASURE: At just 168cm, many thought that Caleb Daniel would be too small to mix it with the best the AFL has to offer, and he was not taken until pick 46 in the 2014 National Draft, despite TAC Cup numbers that suggested he could be an elite player. The Bulldogs showed faith in him, though, and Daniel has repaid that in spades, playing 10 games in his first season and all but two in 2016, to finish runner-up in the 2016 NAB AFL Rising Star award. He was a solid contributor throughout the finals, with a standout performance in the elimination final against West Coast at Subiaco.

GETTING THE JOB DONE: While Jason Johannisen may have gained the most metres and plaudits for his performance in the Grand Final, there was another Bulldog who had just as many touches as 'JJ', and whose work was also pivotal to the win. Jack Macrae's name doesn't hit the headlines as often as those of Stringer and Bontempelli but, week in week out, you will find him in the list of the Bulldogs' best players. Macrae had no fewer than 20 touches in any of the games he played this year and his 33 in the Grand Final went a long way to ensuring the Dogs' victory.

THE BIG MEN FLY: Jordan Roughead gets his hands on the ball ahead of teammate Fletcher Roberts and three Swans, the grimaces on all faces betraying the effort required to win each contest in a Grand Final.

WHEN IT MATTERS MOST: After a strong start to the season, Jake Stringer struggled with a shoulder injury and form at times in the latter half of the season. But after spending a couple of weeks at VFL level he returned for the finals and had an impact when needed. His three goals against Hawthorn in the semi-final—two in the vital third term—were crucial and his last-quarter goal in the Grand Final set the Dogs towards premiership victory.

ONE STEP CLOSER: Liam Picken roars with delight after kicking a goal to give the Bulldogs a seven-point lead in the final term of the Grand Final. Ten minutes later, he kicked another to seal the premiership.

THAT'S IT! OR IS IT? Jason
Johannisen celebrates what
appears to be the match-winning
goal late in the last quarter of
the Grand Final. The goal umpire
signalled a major, but before the
ball was bounced in the centre the
video umpire ruled that the ball had
been touched on the line and the
score was altered to a behind. It was
a moment that could have unsettled
the inexperienced Bulldogs, but
they held their nerve and Tom Boyd
ensured victory with a stunning long
goal a few minutes later.

CAPACITY CROWD: The official capacity of the MCG is 100,024. The 43 who didn't show up for the Grand Final missed a game for the ages. The official attendance of 99,981 was the second-highest at a Western Bulldogs match, behind only the 1961 Grand Final against Hawthorn, which attracted 107,935 fans when the stadium's configuration was significantly different. The scoreboard shows the Western Bulldogs ahead by nine points with only minutes to go, but Bulldogs fans didn't feel the game was won until Tom Boyd kicked his 'goal for the ages' very soon after.

THE MOMENT: With five minutes remaining in the last quarter, the Bulldogs led by just nine points and the Grand Final hung in the balance. Sydney superstar Lance Franklin grabbed a loose ball near the centre of the ground, ready to launch the Swans forward. Enter Dale Morris, whose defensive efforts all day had been heroic. 'Mozz' dragged Franklin to the ground, the ball spilling free to be picked up by Tom Boyd. Franklin could only look on helplessly as Boyd launched a long bomb from inside the centre square. The ball pitched in the goal square, pausing for dramatic effect, before bisecting the big sticks, virtually sealing a Bulldogs' premiership.

COMING OF AGE: Tom Boyd celebrates the goal that sealed the 2016 premiership with teammate Toby McLean. Boyd came to the Bulldogs at the end of the 2014 season in a deal that had many shaking their heads. Injury hampered his progress along the way and lingering doubts remained for some, but he cast those aside with an outstanding finals series which culminated in a Grand Final performance that earned him seven votes and third place in the Norm Smith Medal poll.

GRACIOUS IN DEFEAT AND VICTORY: Luke Beveridge gratefully accepts the congratulations of Sydney coach John Longmire. Undoubtedly devastated by a second Grand Final loss in four years, Longmire was nevertheless only too willing to acknowledge the masterful efforts of the premiership coach and team.

PREMIERS

Against all odds, the Bulldogs took on the Sydney Swans, seasoned finals campaigners who once again topped the ladder in 2016, and beat them in an epic Grand Final that will live long in the memories of all those who witnessed it, not just Bulldogs' fans.

The Western Bulldogs' 2016 premiership is the culmination of, and reward for, years of hard work, commitment and dedication. Not only in the two years since the watershed moment of October 2014 that saw Luke Beveridge and Bob Murphy take the lead, but the years—decades—of effort that came before.

It is just reward for the efforts of Irene Chatfield, who spearheaded the fundraising campaign that saved the Bulldogs from being swallowed up by Fitzroy in 1989; for all the fans who filled those 1989 cans with coins and cash and have continued to barrack their hearts out through thick and thin; for all the players who have toiled, without reward, for 62 years; for the efforts of David Smorgon and Peter Gordon, the only two people to occupy the president's chair since that dogged campaign to save the club; for the efforts of Simon Dalrymple and Jason McCartney, who have put together a playing list the envy of the AFL, and all the unheralded support staff.

This premiership is for all of them—in this highly professional era, it's not just about those who carry the club's values onto the field each week.

But, for the 22 premiership players of 2016 they will take away something even more spiritual: they will be deemed immortals, just like Charlie Sutton's famous 1954 band.

This premiership is for all of them, and all of us.

THE PRESENTATION: The mountain has been conquered and the celebrations begin—some spontaneous, some organised. After the presentation of the Premiership Cup, players and coach pose for a team photo as streamers in team colours are shot from a cannon. This has become a modern AFL tradition.

SIREN: The final siren has sounded and a 62-drought has been broken. Caleb Daniel—having already removed his helmet, a permanent part of his game-day uniform since he was nine years old—joins Shane Biggs, Marcus Bontempelli, Lachie Hunter, Tory Dickson and the rest of the pack in premiership celebration.

MORE THAN ANYONE: A moment that will go down in sporting folklore. Coach Luke Beveridge hands over the Jock McHale Medal he received as premiership coach to Bob Murphy. "You deserve it more than anyone," he said before placing the medal around Murphy's neck. Murphy returned the medal the next day, and Beveridge promptly donated it to the Bulldogs Museum.

GENERATIONAL JUBILATION:
Unbridled, passionate joy adorns the
faces of Bulldog captains Bob Murphy
and Easton Wood as they raise a
premiership club on behalf of the club
for the first time since 1954. Looking
on, equally delighted, are coach Luke
Beveridge and former Footscray
Brownlow Medallist John Schultz.
Schultz had been a member of the
Dogs' last Grand Final side—a losing
one—in 1961. Still an active member
of the Bulldogs' inner sanctum, he
was more than thrilled to see his
successors go one step further.

A CELEBRATORY DRINK: Betraying his basketball background, Marcus Bontempelli emulates the American tradition of giving the premiership winning coach a 'Gatorade shower'. Luke Beveridge, midway through a television interview when given his soaking, took the gesture in good grace.

IT'S YOURS: Players get around 'JJ' the moment after the 'Voice of Football'—Craig Willis—has announced, "The winner of the 2016 Norm Smith Medal is ... Jason Johannisen". Johannisen polled 10 votes to finish two clear of Sydney's Josh Kennedy, with Bulldogs Tom Boyd and Liam Picken polling seven and five votes.

PREMIERSHIP DASH: Jason Johannisen was destined to play rugby. Born in Johannesburg, Johannisen emigrated from South Africa to Australia with his family as a child and settled in Perth where he showed promise with rugby union side the Southern Lions. Fortunately, a footy-loving cousin introduced him to Australian Rules and the rest, as they say, is history. Johannisen's evasive skills and blistering pace saw him climb the ranks to play in a premiership with East Fremantle Colts. Spotted by Bulldogs' recruiting officer Simon Dalrymple, Johannisen was rookie-listed by the Dogs in 2011 and upgraded to the senior list in 2012. He took some time to establish himself but since playing in the Dogs' 2014 VFL premiership side he has been a permanent member of the AFL side. His dash off half-back and long, penetrating kicks have become his signatures and both were in full evidence on Grand Final day, his 865 metres gained more than any other player on the field. His performance netted him the Norm Smith Medal as best player on the ground.

CAPTAIN MY CAPTAIN: Easton Wood and Bob Murphy laugh almost disbelievingly as they revel in the fact that they have led the Dogs to a flag.

PRECIOUS MOMENT: Captain Easton Wood shares a special moment with his mother Fiona, the pair reflecting on the Bulldogs' momentous achievement. Despite the tyranny of distance, the two maintain regular contact, Fiona regularly sending photos to her son of the family property in Gnotuk, in south-west Victoria.

THIS BELONGS TO US ALL: Luke Dahlhaus is only too happy to share a moment with friends and fans as the players do a lap of honour after the Grand Final presentations.

A FAMILY AFFAIR: Liam Picken pose for a photo with his wife Annie and children Malachy, Delphi and Cheska after the Grand Final presentations. It's highly unlikely the photographer would have needed to shout, "Smile!"

FAN-TASTIC!: Matthew Boyd proudly shows off his premiership medallion to young Bulldogs fans after the Grand Final. The veteran midfielder has reinvented himself as a running defender under coach Luke Beveridge and, despite speculation about his future when his form waned slightly in the middle of 2016, Boyd finished the season so strongly that he was named in the 2016 All Australian side. He carried that form into the finals and his 27-touch effort in the Grand Final put him among the Dogs' best. He signed on for his 15th season at Whitten Oval a fortnight after the Grand Final.

VICTORY FROLIC: About three quarters of the way through the players' victory lap, skipper Easton Wood took a sudden turn away from the boundary line and made a beeline for the club logo on the 50-metre arc. His sprint ended as he collapsed joyously on to the turf logo, flapping his arms and legs from side to side, throwing red, white and blue streamers into the air like a child in heaven. What was a private captain's moment of celebration was witnessed and cheered by thousands of euphoric fans in the stands.

WRITTEN IN INK: Clay Smith burst on to the AFL season with a stunning four-goal debut against West Coast in round one of 2012, but has endured more than his fair share of heartbreak since, undergoing three knee reconstructions. Throughout the heartbreak, Smith never once dropped his head, each time working harder than ever to get back to full fitness and rejoin his teammates on the field of battle. He returned for the Bulldogs' thrilling four-point SCG win over Sydney in round 15 and has not looked back since. His four goals against GWS in the preliminary final went a long way towards taking the Dogs into the Grand Final, and his late third-quarter goal on the big day gave his team a lead it would not relinquish.

THE ODD COUPLE: Unheralded and seemingly unobtrusive, Joel Hamling and Fletcher Roberts are now premiership players. Hamling spent several seasons at Geelong, unable to break into the powerful Cats' lineup. He was picked up by the Bulldogs after being delisted by Geelong in 2014 but remained only a bit-part player until late in 2016 when he secured a permanent spot in defence, excelling against all-comers throughout the finals, magnificently blunting the highly dangerous Lance Franklin in the Grand Final. Hamling looked to have usurped Roberts for a defensive role late in the season, but an achilles injury to Matt Suckling saw Roberts regain a place alongside Hamling in the preliminary final and Grand Final, and the pair stood up magnificently in the backline.

THE SPOILS OF VICTORY: For the first time in season 2016, the coaching staff can relax and enjoy a great all-of-club victory. BACK (L-R): Paul Groves (Women's Coach), Stewart Edge (Development Coach), Craig Bain (Match Day Assistant), Joel Corey (Assistant Coach), MIDDLE (L-R): Daniel Giansiracusa (Assistant Coach), Chris Maple (Head of Development), Ashley Hansen (VFL coach), Steven King (Assistant Coach), Jamie Maddocks (Development Coach), FRONT (L-R): Luke Beveridge (Senior Coach), Rohan Smith (Assistant Coach), Denis Bicer (Head of Communications).

THAT'S HOW YOU DO IT, DAD: Tom and Tony Liberatore celebrate the premiership that eluded 'Libba' senior in this 283-game career with the Dogs. Tony played in three losing preliminary finals, including a heartbreaker in 1997 which saw him kick what many thought was the sealing goal. The goal umpire signalled it as a behind, though, and the Bulldogs were overrun by Adelaide, falling just two points short of a Grand Final berth. Tom felt no burden of history as he overcame the disappointment of missing the entire 2015 season through injury to play a key role in the Dogs' burying the preliminary-final hoodoo, and then breaking the premiership drought.

BULLDOG ROYALTY: Isabella, Chris, Sascha and Oliver Grant share a special moment in their lives, after the Grand Final win. Undoubtedly the best 105th draft pick to ever play the game, Chris Grant—described by Doug Hawkins as a Rolls-Royce player— had an outstanding career with the Bulldogs. He became the youngest player in history to kick 50 goals in a season in his first year at the Whitten Oval at the age of just 17. From there, Grant simply got better as his career progressed. He came within a whisker of winning the Brownlow Medal in both 1996 and 1997, was All-Australian three times, won two Charles Sutton Medals, captained the side for five seasons and was inducted into the Australian Football Hall of Fame in 2012. Since retiring he has served as non-executive football director and this year was to the newly created full-time management role of Director of Football.

IN FULL VOICE: The players let out yet another victorious roar as they are presented to adoring fans at the post-match function. (L-R: Bob Murphy, Joel Hamling, Zaine Cordy, Easton Wood, Tom Liberatore, Jack Macrae, Clay Smith, Luke Dahlhaus).

BROUGHT TO YOU BY ... The four biggest financial benefactors of the Western Bulldogs—Peter Gordon, Garry Johnson, Alan Johnstone and Susan Alberti—celebrate the achievement of a lifetime dream on the MCG with the Western Bulldogs board of directors. Lapping it up (from left next to Garry Johnson) are Kylie Watson-Wheeler, Mark Evans, Levent Shevski, Jo Parr (executive assistant to managing director Gary Kent), Peter Gordon, Chris Nolan, Susan Alberti, Gary Kent, Alan Johnstone and Fiona McGauchie. (Football director Matthew Croft was off celebrating with his real friends.)

PRESIDENTIAL SINGALONG: Peter Gordon and David Smorgon belt out 'It's a long way to the top if ya wanna rock'n'roll' for celebrating fans at the Punt Road end after the Grand Final. Gordon took on the role of president after Footscray staved off extinction in 1989, handing the reins over to Smorgon at the end of 1996. Under Smorgon's tenure, the club was rebranded as the Western Bulldogs and began a new era of on-field prosperity. When Gordon took over the presidency in 2012, he promised Smorgon that should the Dogs make it to the premiership podium, he would make sure Smorgon was on the field to enjoy the moment. It's unclear whether the singalong was part of the bargain.

FANS, FAMILY, COMMUNITY

On the back of every Western Bulldogs player's jumper, just above their number, are the letters F.F.C. These letters acknowledge the more than 130 years that the Bulldogs were known as the Footscray Football Club.

But those letters could equally well represent three things that are of great importance to the club: Fans. Family. Community.

It takes 22 players to run out on to the field each week to make a game of footy, but without the fans—themselves a family and a community—there would be no reason to play the game.

The fans celebrate and suffer through the joy of victory and the heartbreak of loss as much as the players do—some would say more so. They come along every week and cheer the Dogs on, win or lose, letting the players know that they have something to play for, even through the darkest of times.

Family and friends perhaps celebrate and suffer most of all. They ride the highest of highs when a player joins them screaming with joy having just kicked the winning goal. And they plumb the depths of despair when a player arrives home to tell them a ruptured ACL will prevent them from playing the game they love for a long 12 months.

Fans, family and community are the reason the Western Bulldogs exist.

The Western Bulldogs have shown commitment to the wider community of the west and beyond, through their *Sons of the West* Men's Health program, *Bulldogs Friendly Schools* and multicultural programs, and consistent engagement with grassroots football and other community partnerships.

The Bulldogs have been leaders in the growth of women's football, driven by the club's long-standing director and vice-president Susan Alberti. Just as the community supports the Bulldogs, the club supports the community.

For all Bulldogs fans and family and the wider Bulldogs community, the 2016 AFL premiership is yours to share, a well-deserved reward for generations of patient support.

ON THE MARCH: The path from Federation Square in Melbourne's CBD to the became a sea of red, white and blue in the hours before the semi-final against Hawthorn and again on Grand Final day.

WE'RE IN THIS TOGETHER:
Two wide-eyed young
fans watch as the Western
Bulldogs take on Adelaide
at Etihad Stadium in round
seven. The Dogs beat the
Crows by 15 points in a
high-scoring 'shoot-out'.

THE POINTY END OF THE SEASON: You're never too young to show your colours, as this youngster demonstrates. The red, white and blue dominated the west in the lead-up to the Grand Final, as fans painted faces, homes, buildings, bowling 'greens' and monuments.

SNARL! With the Western Bulldogs in as strong a position as the club has been on and off the field, these three youngsters may never have to endure what it feels like to experience a multi-generational premiership drought.

THOSE THAT CAME BEFORE US:
Matthew Croft addresses the Bulldog faithful at Federation Square before the 'March to the 'G' on the night of the second semi-final against Hawthorn. An extremely reliable full-back, Croft played 186 games for the Dogs between 1991 and 2004, and was a member of the sides that fell just short of a Grand Final in 1997 and 1998.

ALL SMILES: Bulldogs' fans had plenty to smile about all through September and in to October with Grand Final day on October 1. The smile on this fan's face before the Bulldogs' win over Hawthorn almost seems to betray contentment. Perhaps he knew what was to come.

BULLDOG POWERBROKER: One of these men wields all the power at the Western Bulldogs. The other one is Peter Gordon. Of course, it all depends on your definition of power. Danny McGinlay (at the president's back) is the power behind the banners that have amused Dogs' fans throughout the season, and rankled an opponent or two. McGinlay's best work may have been in the preliminary final: "OUR CLUB WAS BORN IN BLOOD AND BOOTS NOT IN AFL FOCUS GROUPS".

ON A ROLL: The Bulldogs, having upset the Eagles at Subiaco a week earlier, were looking to get on a finals roll with victory over Hawthorn at the MCG in week two of the finals and the fans came out in their thousands to help the Dogs get over the line.

FACING UP TO IT: Face painted red, white and blue, this fan was one of thousands who joined the 'March to the G' before the second semi-final against Hawthorn.

THERE'S NO DISGUISING MY ALLEGIANCE: This fan demonstrates the lengths to which some will go to proudly display their commitment to the cause.

PUT YOUR HOUSE ON IT: Bulldogs' fans were swept up with the emotion of the team's charge towards a flag and they found no shortage of ways to express their support. We're unsure whether this is in the real estate agents' guide to adding value to your home! Pictured from left to right outside their house are Buddy the dog, Charlize Elisaia, Josh Moore, Belinda Youl and Saito Elisaia, with Venu Elisaia in front.

THE DOGFATHER: In just his second season as an AFL coach, Luke Beveridge has very much endeared himself to Doggies' fans, who have found novel ways of throwing their support behind him, using clever banners and signs such as this one.

WE 'WIL' REVERSE THE CURSE: Comedian Wil Anderson became convinced the Bulldogs could reverse the curse of Footscray's Grand Final loss to Hawthorn in '61 and turn it into victory against the Hawks in the '16 semi-final. He was right.

THE TEAM OF THE MIGHTY WEST: It isn't just the 22 who run out on Grand Final day that make up the premiership team, it's the entire playing squad. These fans found a way to acknowledge them all.

REMEMBERING CHARLIE: Charlie Sutton died in June 2012 but he will live forever in the hearts of all Bulldogs as the man who took the club to its first VFL flag as captain-coach in 1954. Charlie remained a stalwart of the club throughout his life, always one of the first to greet the players when they entered the dressing rooms. He was aged 88 when he died, and had endured a losing Grand Final and seven losing preliminary finals after his glorious September day.

NOT SITTING ON THE FENCE: The residents of this household left passersby in no doubt as to their allegiances during the Western Bulldogs' finals campaign.

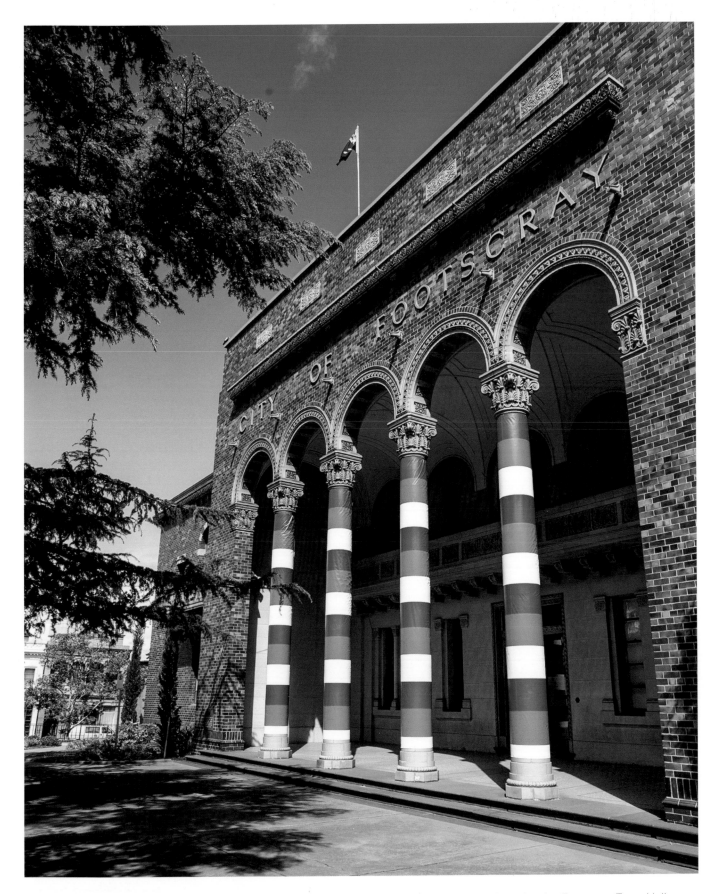

RETURN TO GLORY: On the night of the 1954 Grand Final, victorious Bulldogs players gathered at the Footscray Town Hall to be presented to the adoring and cheering throng of thousands, who had gathered to celebrate the Doggies' first flag after 30 seasons in the League. Sixty-two years later, the old building was again decked out in red, white and blue, this time in anticipation of a second premiership.

A-SPIRE-ING TO GREATNESS: The Victorian Arts Centre's famous spire was lit up in alternating red, white and blue in the days before and after the Bulldogs' premiership win.

MY MAMA SAID, "BE MORE BULLDOG!" Houses, shops and buildings of all description were adorned with red, white and blue as Footscray and the rest of the West got behind the Dogs in their march to a premiership.

BOWLING ALONG TO A PREMIERSHIP: Only a five-minute drive from Whitten Oval, the Rosamond Bowling Club found a unique way to get behind the Doggies during the finals, turning its green into a 'red, white and blue'!

PROUD PARTNERS: Victoria University has worked closely with the Western Bulldogs since forming a partnership in the 1980s, with internationally renowned sport scientists working side by side with the Bulldogs' coaching, medical and performance teams to develop players' skills and fitness in a structured research program. The university is also the major sponsor of the Bulldogs' VFL team, Footscray.

A FITTING FINALE: Who better to close our celebration of a wonderful season than Irene Chatfield, who threw her heart and soul into the campaign that helped save the Bulldogs from extinction in 1989. The 2016 premiership is just reward for her efforts, and all those like her. She couldn't #BEMOREBULLDOG!!!

A PREMIERSHIP SEASON BY THE NUMBERS

1
Norm Smith Medallist:
Jason Johannisen

1
Jock McHale Medallist:
Luke Beveridge

1
Charles Sutton Medallist
(club best and fairest):
Marcus Bontempelli

2
All Australians: Marcus
Bontempelli, Matthew Boyd

2
Times the Bulldogs
won finals out of Victoria,
a feat not done before

3
Wins of 50 points or more

4
Finals wins in a row,
a feat matched only
by Adelaide in 1997

7
The ladder position from
which no other team has
won the premiership

19
Wins from 26 matches
(a club record)

22
Points: The winning
Grand Final margin

39
Players who represented
the team in premiership
matches this season

42
Goals kicked by Jake
Stringer, the most by
a Bulldog in 2016

55
Years since the Bulldogs
last played in a Grand Final

62
Years since the club
last won a premiership

65
Points: the greatest
winning margin of the
season, in round one
versus Fremantle

123
Points: the highest score
of the season, in round
seven versus Adelaide

297
Behinds kicked
for the season

324
Goals kicked for the season

719
Disposals for Lachie
Hunter, more than
any other Bulldog

2241
Total points for

36,711
Average crowd at
the club's games

99,981
Grand Final attendance
(the second-highest
in the club's history)

954,503
Total attendance across
the club's 26 matches

4.089
Million viewers of the
Grand Final on the Seven
Network. Only three other
games have had more TV
viewers: the Grand Finals
of 1996, 2005 and 2006

The Slattery Media Group,
Level 39 / 385 Bourke Street, Melbourne, Victoria, 3000.

First published by The Slattery Media Group, 2016.
Text copyright © The Slattery Media Group.

Prints of photos published in *Against All Odds*
can be purchased at aflphotos.com.au.

The publisher wishes to thank the Western Bulldogs Football Club
for its support with this publication.

National Library of Australia
Cataloguing-in-Publication entry

Creator: Gigacz, Andrew, author.
Title: Against all odds: a pictorial record of the
      Western Bulldogs' history-making season 2016
      edited by Geoff Slattery,
      Andrew Gigacz, author,
      Chris Downey, designer.
ISBN: 9780958528603 (paperback)
Subjects: Australian Football League.
      Western Bulldogs (Football team)
      Australian football--Tournaments.
      Australian football--Competitions.
      Australian football teams--Victoria--History.
Other Creators/Contributors: Slattery, Geoff, editor.

Group Publisher: Geoff Slattery
Project Manager: Marlo Mercuri
Editor: Geoff Slattery
Writer: Andrew Gigacz
Sub-Editor: Stephen Howell
Designer: Chris Downey

Printed by Mercedes Waratah, Melbourne.

www.slatterymedia.com